Clean Eati

Amazingly Delicious Recipes To JumpStart Your Weight Loss, Increase Energy and Feel Great!

Sara Banks

Smashwords Edition

Smashwords Edition, License Notes

Table of Contents

An Introduction to Clean Eating

What is clean eating? Clean eating is incorporating fresh food and all other food groups into your diet. Foods you should also consider buying when doing your food shop are products that have gone through minimal processing and contain little to no additives that are preferably organic or locally grown. Also, try to cook as much at home with fresh ingredients as possible or if you go to work try and make yourself a packed lunch the night before by adding healthy snacks such as; apples, grapes, nuts and oranges.

Processed foods that come in ready to eat form are very bad for your health as these types of products have a lot of preservatives to sustain shelf life and other additives such as; GMO's which have been proven to be bad for your health as chemicals and your natural body don't really mix so this artificial form of 'natural' food will give you no benefits, as the nutrients won't be absorbed by the body. They also can cause gluten disorders which a lot of people have intolerance to today. Therefore, the best food items to choose from are organic.

Eating clean doesn't just consist of eating raw food in moderate quantities, but also should consist of a healthy balanced diet by including all the food groups. To get the best choice choose the organic label as opposed to the natural label. As the government are stricter on the organic label.

Eating too much of a good thing and too much of a bad thing are both unhealthy ways to eat, as your body needs balance, instead eat a bit of everything that amounts in small quantities throughout the day; fruit and veg, starchy foods, milk and dairy, protein and fatty food.

The word diet and losing weight makes you think of what? Eating a salad every couple of hours or water based detoxifier, right? Well, that's the wrong thing to do because it's not healthy! Eating fresh and losing weight can go hand in hand when you make the correct food choices, which will keep you nourished but not stuffed with the wrong foods that your body will want to continue eating until you supplement it with enough nutrients to keep it functioning. Also, if you are looking to lose weight and tone up then exercise is the way to go; take a 30 min run every day or do cardio; pushups, lunges and star jumps.

Chapter 1: How to Adopt a Clean Eating Diet

Firstly, before I get right into this section, it is important to understand that for this regime to work you must be fully committed to this diet.

The benefits of adopting a clean diet are; you'll be more fulfilled and less hungry, I know this because whenever I eat more than usual one day I'm usually just as hungry the next day too, as my stomach has expanded to meet the amount of food I was eating the previous day thus adapting itself for today and making my appetite as big as yesterday's.

If you train yourself to eat a certain way, your body will get used to it, and eating the right amounts will leave you feeling less hungry, your health will reflect in your energy levels by it being increased, your skin will start to glow and your blood cells will renew itself with healthy nutrients rather than toxins infusing into the blood and tissues from bad processed food. Furthermore, bones renew themselves every 10 years and what you eat vastly affects the health of those new bones that you are contributing to by what you eat because your bone tissue absorbs it.

Suppress your wants and give into your needs, you'll be doing yourself a favor and your future self will thank you. When it comes to eating healthier, quality trumps quantity.

Eat a balanced diet

Eating healthily will reduce the risk of some types of cancers and diseases, not only that but if you get sick often, it most likely isn't due to the environment you are exposed to but your current diet because many fresh foods have bacteria fighting properties in them. For example; eating citrusy fruits like; kiwis, oranges, lemons and limes (in your water/fresh juices) give acidity to your stomach, liver and bladder which helps fight ulcers and infections if and when they occur.

Proteins are a vital part of our diet to build and maintain muscle and body weight. So, instead of going for the most obvious proteins; red meats, steaks etc. change it to plant based proteins or sustainable and environmentally friendly fish as this doesn't only benefit the environment but also your health. Fish is also known as brain food because of its omega 3 & 6 content, however bare in mind the type of fish you choose at the store because most fish have a higher content of omega 6 and less of the omega 3, which most people are deficient in. Fish with a high content of omega 3 include; kipper fillets and sardines.

In this day and age eating organic is all the craze and this is why; strict laws have been put in place about the labelling of organic products which keeps profit crazed companies from adding chemicals to your food. Don't be fooled by a product that states that it has all natural ingredients because when a consumer reads 'natural' on a product label they expect plant-based ingredients only, little do they know the food could be grown with pesticides as it is cheaper than natural fertilizer. Labelling regulations on the word 'natural' is less strict because there is no more meaning to natural.

Fun fact: What we eat has an impact on our brains. Did you know that bananas contain 10 milligrams of dopamine, an awesome mood booster for the brain? Dark chocolate, packed with polyphenol, is also known to boost serotonin, a neurotransmitter that many antidepressants greatly target.

Do not snack after dinner

If you get hungry; grab a piece of fruit. Smart, simple and healthy choices like replacing soda with homemade juice (made from fresh ingredients, which can be store in the fridge), baking homemade vegetables like; pumpkin, squash or carrot strips, instead of eating packaged crisps that are heavy in saturated fat, are a great low fat choice. When eating out, ordering a side of salad instead of fries will suppress the urge to snack as it does not fluctuate blood cholesterol levels making your body crave more.

Avoid highly processed and sugary foods

They will bring you nothing but a physiological high but a physical low as your body has to work really hard to balance your body levels again. So, when blood sugar is high it causes you to want to continue eating to stay on the high, so it doesn't fluctuate body levels from a high to a low dramatically.

Pre-packaged foods like ready meals, that you can just bung in the microwave as is, is the worst kind of processed food there is because they add so many more chemicals that are toxins to your body in order to make it look more appealing and to sustain flavor and durability while in the store.

Unhealthy food also takes a toll on your metabolism to get rid of excess in the body from food that it doesn't need by storing it as fat. So, if you eat too many processed foods the metabolism will start to deteriorate as it cannot keep up with the workload and as your metabolism fails on you so will the balance in body levels, the metabolism tries to sustain.

Chapter 2: Clean Eating Tips and Food Groups

Clean eating is a great way to refresh you current eating habits, if you follow this regime you will end up feeling satisfied after every meal and won't be reaching for those unhealthy snacks and you'll soon realize that it's unnecessary and actually you feel much better without it. The recipes are all very simple and the ingredients are easily accessible. So, it is very easy to include more of those foods into your diet.

Also, eating well and losing weight go hand in hand because you don't need to cut out all food groups as each you will need for a healthy balanced diet. The carbohydrates group has some very healthy and filling food so you need to eat those more than the rest of the food groups. Additionally, when you eat healthy you don't have to look out for calories as much as you may have for packaged or processed foods because there are no additives and therefore, you also won't put on a lot of weight because fresh food has a lot of water content and healthy unsaturated fats.

What to eat

Good for snacks;

Nuts: are very healthy for your heart and provide omega-3.

- Almonds; has more calcium than any other nut and is rich in fiber, vitamin E and has anti- inflammatory properties.

- Walnuts; contain antioxidants and reduce the risk of diabetes.

- Pistachios; are anti-inflammatory, give healthy strong hair and boosts hair growth.

- Peanuts; are high in folate, essential for brain function.

- Brazil nuts; are full of selenium, which protects against cancer.

Avoid salted or roasted nuts.

Fish: contain omega-6 and 3.

- Salmon; is dense in nutrients and supply an excellent source of quality protein. It protects your eyes and helps you sleep.

- Sea Bass; is an excellent provider of protein, selenium, omega-3 fatty acids and vitamin B-6 and B-12.

- Tuna; reduces risk of heart disease, cognitive decline and inflammation.

- Mackerel; controls and levels blood pressure and improves cognitive function.

- Halibut; is a good source of folic acid, vitamin B-12 and B-6 and assists in lowering cholesterol.

- Cod; is abundant in lean protein, is heart-healthy and keeps hair and skin healthy.

- Prawns; reduces risk of cancer, heart-disease and arthritis. Rich in vitamins and is low in fats.

- Anchovies; are essential for growth and helps maintain strong bones. Also, rich in iron.

Poultry: provide protein and vitamins B & E, zinc, iron and magnesium.

- Turkey (skinless); is a great source of vitamin B6 and niacin, lowers cholesterol, strengthens immune system and provides selenium.

- Chicken (skinless); is a natural anti-depressant, metabolism booster, is rich in phosphorus which helps the nervous system function and keeps teeth and bones strong.

- Duck; contains every amino acid needed in your diet, vitamin B-5, maintains healthy tissue and skin.

- Quail Eggs; are great at removing heavy metals from your system and toxins from the blood. They also rid your bodily functions of stones found in the bladder, liver and kidneys.

Dairy: helps improve bone health and promotes healthy bones and teeth from the nutrient calcium.

- Yoghurt; contains healthy bacteria which helps repair damaged skin cells, is loaded with vitamins and stops high blood pressure. Choose non-fat.

- Cheese; provides nutrients; calcium, protein, phosphorus, zinc and vitamin B-12 and A. Choose cottage cheese, cheddar, goat's, mozzarella, brie, ricotta and parmesan.

- Milk; promotes healthy bones and calcium in milk is easily absorbed in the body. Choose skimmed or low-fat; cows, goats and soya milk.

Vegetables: are rich in potassium useful for balancing blood pressure levels and is are also rich in fiber, folic acid and vitamins C and A.

Choose fresh broccoli, spinach, cauliflower, peas, tomatoes, garlic, peppers and more.

Fruits: rich in many vitamins, nutrients and contain superfoods such as strawberries, dark grapes, blueberries, red berries that have extra benefits.

Choose bananas, grapes, strawberries and other berries, peaches, apples, oranges, avocados, kiwi, pomegranate and more.

Carbohydrates: don't make you gain weight unless eaten in excessive quantities. There are some carbs that are very beneficial to you in this food group.

Choose whole grain bread, rice and pasta. Quinoa, barley, bulgur, sweet potatoes.

Fats and oils: healthy oils contain omega-3 and are rich in nutrients.

Extra virgin olive oil is great for cooking and on uncooked foods like salad, raw virgin coconut oil is the best cooking oil and avocado oil is healthy as well.

What to avoid or eat less often

Consume less processed foods which are added with chemicals and are highly refined, full of sugars, starchy foods, salt and saturated/trans-fats. Replace each unhealthy food with something healthy listed above. If you are struggling to adopt this technique right away, minimize slowly by removing one bad thing each day. You can have it occasionally or best of all, try to avoid it completely.

Dairy: full-fat ice cream, processed cheese sauce, pasteurized process cheese; velveeta, cheese whiz, laughing cow and dairy lea.

Legumes: Peanut butter, chocolate spread; Nutella, roasted or salted nuts.

Vegetables: fried potatoes.

Snacks: chips, cakes, energy bars, candy and breakfast bars.

Sugar and Artificial sweeteners: maple syrup, corn syrup, fructose and processed honey.

Fruits high in fructose: like dried fruit and cantaloupe.

Avoid all deeply fried foods and fast food.

Breakfast Recipes

Berry Porridge Bowl

Makes 2 Servings

Ingredients:

-5 tbsp. porridge oats

-400ml skimmed milk

-Fresh berries, of your choice

-100ml natural Greek-style yogurt

Instructions:

1.) Heat oats in a saucepan with milk and cook over a medium to low heat, stir occasionally for about 5 mins until it turns thick.

2.) Pour the porridge into bowls and spoon the yogurt on top.

3.) Then pile on the fresh berries and serve immediately.

Nutritional value: calories: 212, protein: 11g, carbohydrates: 48g, fat: 3g, saturates: 1g, fiber: 4g, sugar: 21g, salt: 0.3g

Multi-Vitamin Smoothie

Makes 2 Servings

Ingredients:

-½ avocado (peeled & quartered)

-1 banana (halved)

-200ml semi-skimmed milk

-1 celery stick

-4 tbsp. low-fat natural yogurt

-syrup (to taste)

Instructions:

1.) Add all the ingredients in a blender and blend until smooth.

2.) If it's too thick add more milk.

3.) Serve cold.

Nutritional value: calories: 65, protein: 3g, carbohydrates: 18g, fat: 2g, saturates: 0g, fiber: 5g, sugar: 9g, salt: 0.3g

Blueberry Pancakes

Makes 15

Ingredients:

-1 cup, plain flour

-1 tsp. cream of tartar

-½ tsp, bicarbonate of soda

-1 tsp, golden syrup

-1 free-range/organic egg

-200ml milk

-unsalted butter, for cooking

-small handful, blueberries

Instructions:

1.) Combine the flour, cream of tartar and bicarbonate of soda together into a mixing bowl. Mix them well with a fork.

2.) Add the golden syrup into the mixing bowl along with the blueberries.

3.) Pour the milk into a measuring jug and break in the egg and mix well with a fork.

4.) Pour most of the milk mixture into the mixing bowl and mix well with a rubber spatula. Steadily add more milk until you get a smooth and thick batter.

5.) Heat a frying pan and coat with a little butter. Then spoon on the mixture, 1 tbsp at a time. Turn them as bubbles start to appear, using a metal spatula. Cook until brown on the second side, and then keep warm on a plate, covered with foil. Repeat until all the batter is used.

Nutritional value: calories: 112, protein: 4, carbohydrates: 17g, fat: 4g, saturates: 1g, fiber: 2g, sugar: 0.2g, salt: 0.6g

Omelette

Makes 2 Servings

Ingredients:

-2 free-range or organic eggs

-3 egg whites,

-1 tsp, olive oil,

-1 red pepper (deseeded & finely chopped.)

-a few slices, bacon (chopped)

-2 spring onions (finely chopped)

-¼ cup, mature cheddar cheese,

Instructions:

1.) Mix the eggs and egg whites in a bowl, add salt and pepper, set aside.

2.) Heat the oil in a medium frying pan and cook the bacon for 5 mins and add red pepper, then cook further for 4 more mins. Pour in the eggs and cook over a medium heat until almost completely set.

3.) Sprinkle on the cheese and continue cooking until melted. If you like it well done cook for a few extra mins. Serve straight from the pan and garnish with spring onions and whole meal toast.

Nutritional value: calories: 110, protein: 12g, carbohydrates: 6g, fat: 24g, saturates: 5g, fiber: 3g, sugar: 0.7g, salt: 1.9g

Scrambled Eggs on Toast

Makes 1 Serving

Ingredients:

-2 organic or free-range eggs

-1 tbsp. crème fraîche

-¼ cup, grated cheddar cheese

-handful chives (finely chopped)

-1 tsp. oil

-2 slices, seeded toast

-1 spring onion (chopped)

Instructions:

1.) Beat together the eggs, crème fraîche, cheddar cheese and chives and season.

2.) Heat oil in a frying pan and add spring onions, cook for a few minutes until soft. Then, add the egg mixture.

3.) Cook on a low heat, while stirring until the eggs have just set. Do not overcook!

4.) Add onto toast.

Nutritional value: calories: 65, protein: 3, carbohydrates: 6g, fat: 3g, saturates: 3g, fiber: 1.5g, sugar: 0g, salt: 0.7g

Cheese Soufflé

Makes 4 Servings

Ingredients:

-50g butter, plus extra for greasing

-25g plain flour, plus extra for dusting

-200ml milk

-300g hard cheese (cut into chunks)

-100ml double cream or crème fraiche

-4 eggs (separated)

-nutmeg (grated)

-pinch of cayenne pepper

Instructions:

1.) Preheat the oven to 390 degrees.

2.) In a saucepan, melt the butter and grease 20cm soufflé dishes with some of it. Then, dust with flour and set aside.

3.) In the saucepan, stir the flour into the remaining melted butter, then sizzle for a min. Gradually pour in milk to form a white sauce and add 2/3 of the cheese. When melted, take off the heat and slightly cool for a minute.

4.) Then, combine the remaining cheese, crème fraîche and egg yolks. Season with cayenne pepper and nutmeg

5.) In a new mixing bowl, whisk the egg whites until they form stiff peaks. Then, fold it into the white sauce and pour into the prepped soufflé dishes.

6.) Bake for 25 mins until raised and has a golden top.

Nutritional value: calories: 410, protein: 22g, carbohydrates: 21g, fat: 27g, saturates: 15g, fiber: 1.5g, sugar: 4.08g, salt: 1.07g

Flapjack

Makes 12

Ingredients:

-¼ cup, mixed dried fruits (raisins, sultanas and currants) (chopped)

-1/3 cup, mixed seeds

-1 ½ cups, oats

-½ cup, light muscovado sugar

-½ cup, unsalted butter

-1/3 cup, golden syrup

Instructions:

1.) Preheat the oven to 320 degrees.

2.) Grease and line with baking parchment paper, a 20cm square cake tin.

3.) Combine dried fruit, seeds and oats into a bowl and mix well.

4.) In a saucepan, add the butter, sugar and golden syrup and cook gently on the stove. Stir until the butter and sugar have melted.

5.) Remove from the heat and mix the dry ingredients into the saucepan until its combined well and have a syrupy coating.

6.) Pour the mixture into the baking tin. Using a spatula, press the mix down and spread evenly. Bake for 20 mins, then leave to cool completely before cutting it into squares.

Nutritional value: calories: 180, protein: 3.7g, carbohydrates: 24.5g, fat: 7.6g, saturates: 1.7g, fiber: 3.8g, sugar: 13g, salt: 0.1g

Applesauce Cookies

Makes 12

Ingredients:

-½ cup, flour

-½ tsp. baking soda

-¼ tsp. salt

-¼ tsp. nutmeg

-½ tsp. cinnamon

-½ cup, quick cook oats

-2/3 cups, raisins

-½ cup, unsweet applesauce

-¼ cup, vegetable oil

-1 free-range egg

-1 tsp. vanilla

-1 tbsp. liquid sweetener

Instructions:

1) Preheat the oven to 375 degrees.

2) Mix the first 6 ingredients together in a bowl.

2) In another bowl mix; applesauce, oil, egg, vanilla and liquid sweetener together.

3) Beat lightly.

4) Combine both dry and wet ingredients together and mix well until moist.

5) Drop teaspoonfuls onto a greased cookie sheet. Making sure the cookie sheet is cold.

6) Bake for 10 minutes or until golden brown.

Nutritional value: calories: 213, protein: 2g, carbohydrates: 30g, fat: 9g, saturates: 2g, fiber: 11g, sugar: 14g, salt: 0.1g

Lunch Recipes

Creamy Asparagus Pasta

Makes 2 Servings

Ingredients:

-4 ½ cups, fusilli

-10 asparagus spears (woody ends removed & cut into lengths)

-Large handful, each of frozen peas

-Zest and juice, ½ lemon

-½ cup, soft cheese

Instructions:

1.) Cook the pasta by the pack instructions.

2.) 2 minutes nearing the end of the cooking time, add peas and asparagus.

3.) Boil everything together for the final 2 mins, then scoop out and reserve a cup of the cooking liquid from the pan before draining.

4.) Return the pasta and veg into the empty pan and add the lemon zest, soft cheese, seasoning and stir in 2-3 tbsp of the cooking liquid to thin the sauce.

5.) Serve hot.

Nutritional value: calories: 623, protein: 24g, carbohydrates: 80g, fat: 27g, saturates: 15g, fiber: 6g, sugar: 8g, salt: 0.3g

Roast Dinner

Makes 4 Servings

Ingredients:

-1 whole chicken

-1 lemon (halved)

-4 tbsp. margarine

-2 tsp. dried mixed herbs

-5 medium potatoes (quartered)

-7 carrots (chopped into 2-3 chunks)

-2 tbsp. extra virgin olive oil

-2 handfuls, frozen peas

-300ml fresh chicken stock

Instructions:

1.) Heat oven to 425 degrees.

2.) Snip the string off the chicken (if it's tied), then place it in a large roasting tin.

3.) Stick both lemon halves into the cavity. Rub the butter, herbs and seasoning all over the chicken. Put the potatoes and carrots around the chicken and drizzle it all with olive oil.

4.) Roast for 20 mins, then turn the oven down to 390 degrees and roast for 50 more mins.

5.) Add the peas and stock into the veggies side of the tin, stir. Then return to the oven for 10 mins more.

Nutritional value: calories: 869, protein: 54g, carbohydrates: 46g, fat: 48g, saturates: 6g, fiber: 6g, sugar: 11g, salt: 1.1g

Sun-dried Tomatoes Couscous

Makes 3 Servings

Ingredients:

-535ml water,

-1 cup, couscous

-1 tbsp. olive oil

-3oz sun-dried tomatoes, from a bag (not kept in oil).

-1oz fresh basil leaves

- half a lemon, juice only

-seasoning, salt and pepper

- Feta (crumbled)

-1 ½ bunches spring onions (chopped)

- 4½ cloves garlic (crushed and chopped)

Instructions:

1.) Place sun-dried tomatoes into a bowl with water. Soak for 30 minutes, until rehydrated. Drain over a bowl, reserving the water. Then, roughly chop the sun-dried tomatoes into little pieces.

2.) Put a medium saucepan on a medium heat. Then, add the reserved water and bring to the boil.

3.) Stir in the couscous.

4.) Remove the pan from heat, then cover using a lid and leave for a couple of minutes. Then, lightly fluff the couscous with a fork.

5.) Meanwhile, heat the olive oil in a wok. Adding the chopped sun-dried tomatoes, garlic, spring onions and sauté for five minutes, until the spring onions are soft.

6.) Combine basil and lemon juice then season, to taste.

7.) Serve right away.

Nutritional value: calories: 380, protein: 12g, carbohydrates: 32g, fat: 15g, saturates: 8g, fiber: 5g, sugar: 3g, salt: 1.5g

Chicken Hot Pot

Serves 4

Ingredients:

-4 tbsp. butter or margarine,

-plus extra for greasing

-1 onion (chopped)

-12 button mushrooms (sliced)

-1/3 cup, plain flour

-500ml fresh chicken stock

-Pinch of mustard powder

-Pinch of nutmeg

-8 broccoli

-250g cooked chicken (sliced)

-garden peas (canned)

-sweetcorn (canned)

-baby carrots (canned)

for the topping:

- knob of butter, melted

-2 large potatoes, sliced into rounds

Instructions:

1.) Preheat oven to 390 degrees.

2.) Grease a medium-sized pie dish.

3.) Place the butter in a medium saucepan and melt over a medium heat.

4.) Add to the pan the onion and leave to cook for 4 mins, stirring occasionally. Place the mushrooms in the saucepan with the onions.

5.) Once almost cooked, mix in the flour, this will then form a paste called a ''roux''.

6.) Now, take the roux off the heat and add the fresh stock steadily, stirring constantly. Once all of it is added, season with pepper, a pinch of nutmeg and mustard powder.

7.) Place the saucepan back onto a medium heat and slowly bring it to the boil, stirring continually. Once the consistency has thickened, place on a very low heat.

8.) Add the cooked chicken strips and vegetables to the sauce and stir well. Pour the chicken filling into the pie dish.

9.) Lay the potatoes on top of the filling and overlap them slightly. Brush the potatoes with a little melted butter and bake for 35 mins or once the potatoes turn golden brown.

Nutritional value: calories: 340, protein: 21g, carbohydrates: 28g, fat: 13g, saturates: 6g, fiber: 3g, sugar: 4g, salt: 1g

Kale Chickpea & Bean Stew

Makes 3 Servings

Ingredients:

-1 ½ carrots (chopped)

-1 ½ sweet bell pepper (chopped)

-2 handfuls of kale

-1 clove of garlic (finely sliced)

-1 butter beans (canned)

-Herbs: thyme, coriander, oregano,

-fresh parsley.

-salt and pepper

-1 celery stick (chopped)

- 1 medium sweet potato (chopped)

-1 onion (chopped)

- 2 chopped tomatoes (canned)

-chickpeas (canned)

-1 glass of water

-drizzle of extra virgin olive oil

Instructions:

1.) In baking pot, add the chopped tomatoes and cook it on low to medium heat, stir and add then vegetables. Add one glass of water at the end and let it simmer for 10 mins on a medium heat.

2.) Meanwhile, wash the kale and separate the leaves from the stalk. Combine the kale leaves to the pot of tomatoes and let it simmer for another 5 mins.

3.) Garnish the stew with herbs and let it simmer for a bit longer to allow the herbs infuse together, adding more flavor to the dish.

Nutritional value: calories: 503, protein: 27g, carbohydrates: 11g, fat: 19g, saturates: 7g, fiber: 8g, sugar: 2g, salt: 1.1g

Aubergine Slider

Makes 4

Ingredients:

-3 tbsp. extra virgin olive oil

-2 aubergines, sliced

-4 tomatoes

-1 ball, mozzarella, sliced

-Basil leaves

Instructions:

1) Preheat the oven to 390 degrees.

2) Grease an oven tray.

3) Place the aubergine slices on the oven tray and drizzle with oil

4) Bake in the oven for 25 mins until softened.

5) Once cooked arrange the tomato and mozzarella on top of the aubergine. Return to oven for another 5 mins or until the cheese has melted. Scatter over some basil leaves. Serve hot.

Nutritional value: calories: 210, protein: 11g, carbohydrates: 6g, fat: 19g, saturates: 7g, fiber: 3g, sugar: 5g, salt: 0.5g

Dinner Recipes

Turkey Casserole

Makes 2 Servings

Ingredients:

-1/2 cup, cooked, enriched noodles

-4 oz. cooked turkey, bite-size pieces

-1/2 cup, green beans, divided

-1/4 cup, canned, sliced mushrooms

-2 tbsp. skim milk

-1 oz. red onion, chopped

-1 tsp. chopped pimento

-¼ tsp. nutmeg

-¼ tsp. sea salt

Instructions:

1) Preheat the oven to 350 degrees.

2) Combine noodles, turkey, 1/4 cup green beans, and mushrooms.

3) Add onion, pimento, nutmeg and salt and pour into a casserole or baking dish.

4) In blender, combine the remaining green beans and milk, mix until smooth.

5) Add green bean sauce to casserole and mix well.

6) Bake for 20 minutes.

Nutritional value: calories: 590, protein: 16g, carbohydrates: 52g, fat: 45g, saturates: 2g, fiber: 3g, sugar: 3g, salt: 1.9g

Crab Cakes

Makes 6 Servings

Ingredients:

-3 tbsp. low-fat mayonnaise

-1 free-range/organic egg

-1 tbsp. mustard

-Juice 1 lemon

-Fresh parsley, chopped

-500g white crabmeat

-4 tbsp. breadcrumbs

-5 tbsp. extra virgin olive oil

for the sauce:

-3 shallots, diced

-3 tbsp. thick double cream

-1 ½ cups, butter, cubed

-1 lemon, juiced

-350ml white wine

Instructions:

1) Preheat oven to 375 degrees.

2) Mix together the mayonnaise, egg, mustard, lemon juice and parsley. Fold crabmeat into the mix, then add the breadcrumbs. Chill for 25 mins then shape into 6 cakes.

3) Heat in a frying pan, heat the olive oil and allow the crab cakes to brown on both sides. Then transfer to the oven for 10 mins or until cooked through.

4) For the sauce: boil the white wine, shallots and thyme until reduced.

5) Add the cream and bring back to the boil. Then, remove from the heat and slowly add the butter, whisking constantly. Complete the sauce by adding fresh lemon juice and season to taste. Serve together.

Nutritional value: calories: 694, protein: 17g, carbohydrates: 10g, fat: 62g, saturates: 29g, fiber: 0g, sugar: 4g, salt: 2.13g

Orzo Meatballs

Makes 4 Servings

Ingredients:

-Handful, fresh basil, chopped

-1 pack, minced beef

-2 garlic cloves, crushed

-1 tbsp. dried oregano

-1 tbsp. extra virgin olive oil

-1 jar, passata

-3 cups, orzo

-parmesan, shavings

Instructions:

1) Mix the basil with the mince, garlic and oregano and roll into 20-24 meatballs.

2) Heat the oil then the meatballs in a frying pan over a high heat and brown each side for 5 mins. Stir in the passata and bring to the boil for 5 mins.

3) Then, turn down to a simmer and cook for another 10 mins.

3) Cook the orzo following pack instructions.

4) Once cooked and drained, scoop and serve. Top with the meatballs, then sprinkle the Parmesan on top and scatter with the reserved basil leaves. Serve immediately.

Nutritional value: calories: 632, protein: 36g, carbohydrates: 65g, fat: 24g, saturates: 9g, fiber: 3g, sugar: 1g, salt: 0.2g

Prawn Style Curry

Makes 4 Servings

Ingredients:

-1 tbsp. vegetable oil

-1 red onion, chopped

-1 tsp. root ginger

-2 tsp. red curry paste

-2 chopped tomatoes, canned

-4 tbsp. coconut milk

-1 pack, frozen prawns

-fresh coriander, chopped

Instructions:

1) Heat the oil in a saucepan. Then, add in the onion and ginger and cook for a few mins until soft.

2) Stir in curry paste, then cook for 1 min more and pour over the chopped tomatoes and coconut milk. Bring to the boil, then leave to simmer for 5 mins.

2) Put in the prawns, then cook for 10 mins more. Serve with plain rice.

Nutritional value: calories: 180, protein: 20g, carbohydrates: 6g, fat: 9g, saturates: 4g, fiber: 1g, sugar: 5g, salt: 0.7g

Cauliflower Cheese

Makes 6 Servings

Ingredients:

-1 large cauliflower, leaves cut and in chunks

-500ml semi-skimmed milk

-4 tbsp. plain flour

-4 tbsp. unsalted butter

-handful cheese, grated

-seasoning

Instructions:

1) Preheat the oven to 425 degrees.

2) Bring a large saucepan of water to the boil and add the cauliflower, then cook for 5 mins until soft. Drain the cauliflower and tip into an ovenproof dish.

3) Bring the pan back on the heat, then add the milk, flour and butter. Whisking it fast as the butter melts and the mixture begins to boil – a sauce will begin to thicken. Whisk for 2 mins while the sauce bubbles and becomes nice and thick. Turn off the heat, stir in half of the cheese and pour over the cauliflower. Scatter over the remaining cheese and breadcrumbs. Serve immediately.

Nutritional value: calories: 250, protein: 13g, carbohydrates: 16g, fat: 15g, saturates: 9g, fiber: 3g, sugar: 8g, salt: 1g

Chicken Kiev

Makes 8 Servings

Ingredients:

-8 chicken breast fillets

-8 tbsp. breadcrumbs

-1 cup, parmesan, grated

-5 organic eggs, beaten

-¾ cup, flour

-paprika, a pinch

-4 tbsp. sunflower oil

For garlic butter center:

-4 garlic cloves, crushed

-¾ cup, unsalted butter, softened

-2 tbsp. fresh parsley, chopped

-½ lemon, squeezed

Instructions:

1) Preheat the oven to 355 degrees.

2) Place all the garlic butter ingredients in a bowl and season well. Mash with a fork until combined, shape into two sausages, using cling film to help you, then wrap and chill until firm. Once chilled, slice each evenly into 8 pieces.

3) Lay the chicken breast on a chopping board and use a sharp knife to make a deep pocket inside the breast, one by one. The simplest way is to push the point of a knife into the fat end, keeping going until halfway into the fillet, but don't cut all it through all the way. Push the 2 slices of butter inside each chicken breast, press to flatten and re-seal with your hands. Return to it later.

4) Meanwhile, mix together the breadcrumbs and parmesan on a plate and tip the eggs into another bowl. On a third plate; stir the flour and paprika with some salt.

5) Going from one plate to another, slide each breast in the flour, then the egg and finally the breadcrumbs, repeating so each Kiev has a double coating, making it extra crispy and will allow the butter to stay inside. Keep in the fridge for at least an hour before cooking or freeze now to prepare for later use.

6) Heat oil in a frying pan on a medium to high heat and fry the Kievs for 3 mins on each side until golden. Transfer them onto a baking tray and cook for the last 20-25 mins until cooked through.

Nutritional value: calories: 549, protein: 30g, carbohydrates: 31g, fat: 35g, saturates: 17g, fiber: 2g, sugar: 2g, salt: 1.02g

Mexican Pot

Makes 2 Servings

Ingredients:

-2 tbsp. avocado oil

-1 onion, finely chopped

-450g pork mince

-4 chopped tomatoes, canned

-3 tbsp. tomato puree

-3 cups, cooked rice

-fresh parsley, chopped

Instructions:

1) Heat oil in a saucepan until hot, then add in the onion and allow it to turn golden, after 5 mins, stirring occasionally. Add mince to the pan and cook until it's no longer pink.

2) Put the tomatoes into the mince and the tomato purée, then give it a good mix and let it come to the boil. Simmer, with the lid covered, for 25 minutes to cook it all through.

3) Add in the rice and let the flavors infuse and garnish with parsley.

Nutritional value: calories: 489, protein: 30g, carbohydrates: 46g, fat: 22g, saturates: 5g, fiber: 3g, sugar: 1g, salt: 1.1g

Dessert Recipes

Apple, Strawberry & Macadamia Crumble

Makes 2 Servings

Ingredients:

-3 apples, cut into thin wedges (keep skin)

-1 tsp. cinnamon

-1 cup, almond flakes

-¼ cup, macadamias

-1 tbsp. chia seeds

-½ cup, coconut oil

-2 tsp. vanilla extract

-14 strawberries (sliced into quarters)

-½ cup, oats

-¼ cup, pumpkin seeds

-3 tbsp. maple syrup or honey

Instructions:

<u>Filling:</u>

1.) Place the strawberries and apples into a steamer basket over a pot of simmering water, sprinkle with cinnamon and place the lid on top.

2.) Simmer for approximately 5 mins or until the apples are soft.

3.) Put the steamed apple and strawberries into a baking dish, spreading the fruit to cover the entire surface of the base of the dish.

Crumble:

1.) Preheat the oven to 320 degrees.

2.) In a bowl, mix together all dry ingredients.

3.) Melt the coconut oil and pour over the dry ingredients. Before mixing it in, add in the liquid sweetener and vanilla extract and stir well.

4.) The crumble mix should form a ball when squeezed together with your palms. If not, add more coconut oil to the ''doughy'' mix.

5.) Spread the crumble mix over the top of the fruit aligned in the baking dish and cover it completely.

6.) Bake for 15 mins or until the crumble turns golden. Serve hot.

Nutritional value: calories: 230, protein: 3g, carbohydrates: 49g, fat: 17g, saturates: 10g, fiber: 3g, sugar: 21g, salt: 0.05g

Panna Cotta with Compote

Makes 4 Servings

Ingredients:

<u>For Panna Cotta:</u>

-3 tsp. gelatine

-2 tbsp water

-520ml soya milk

-1 lemon, zested

-2 tbsp. caster sugar

<u>For Compote:</u>

-8 ripe peaches, stoned and halved

-150ml water

-¼ cup, caster sugar

-1 vanilla pod, split and scooped

Instructions:

<u>For Panna Cotta:</u>

1.) Add the gelatine to water and soak for 7 mins.

2.) Meanwhile, in a saucepan add soya milk, zest, sugar and vanilla pod. Next you will want to heat until the liquid just about comes to slight boil, then carefully remove from the heat and slowly stir in the gelatine.

3.) Cool for about 12-15 mins. Then you want to strain the mixture of mile and split between 4 ramekins. Then you want to cover with cling film and refrigerate for 1 ½ hours until it sets.

For Compote:

1.) In a saucepan, combine caster sugar and water and heat until the sugar has dissolved.

2.) Add the peaches and cook over a very gentle heat for about 12-15 mins or so until the peaches are semi soft, then leave to cool for a bit. Happily serve along with the panna cotta.

Nutritional value: calories: 134, protein: 6g, carbohydrates: 38g, fat: 3g, saturates: 0g, fiber: 3g, sugar: 21g, salt: 0.1g

Pear Tarte Tatin

Makes 8 Servings

Ingredients:

-8 pears, cored, peeled and halved

-1/2 cup, caster sugar

-1/3 cup, unsalted butter

-500g puff pastry

-3 cardamom pods

-1 cinnamon stick

-2 star anise

Instructions:

1.) In a saucepan, tip the sugar, butter, star anise, cardamom and cinnamon and place over a high heat, cook until bubbling. Shake the pan and stir the buttery sauce until it separates and the sugar caramelizes.

2.) Lay the pears in the pan, then cook in the sauce for 10-12 mins, until completely caramelized. Caramelize as much as you can, they don't burn. Then set the pears aside.

3.) Heat oven to 390 degrees.

4.) Meanwhile, roll out the pastry to 2cm in thickness. Using a plate slightly larger than the top of the pan, cut out a circle, then make the edges thinner by pressing them down.

5.) When the pears have cooled slightly, arrange them in the pan.

6.) Rest the cinnamon stick on the top in the center, with the cardamom pods scattered around it.

7.) Drape the pastry over the pears, then tuck the edges down the sides of the pan and under the fruit. Pierce the pastry a few times with a fork and bake for 15 mins. If juice bubbles up the side of the pan, pour it off at this stage.

8.) Reduce the oven to 360 degrees and bake for 15 mins more until the pastry is golden. Leave it to cool in the dish for 10 mins until placing it on a plate.

Nutritional value: calories: 385, protein: 6g, carbohydrates: 46g, fat: 22g, saturates: 11g, fiber: 3g, sugar: 24g, salt: 0.8g

Tiramisu

Makes 6 Servings

Ingredients:

-570ml double cream

-1 cup, mascarpone

-75ml Marsala

-5 tbsp. caster sugar

-300ml hot coffee

-1 pack sponge fingers

-¼ bar, dark chocolate

-2 tsp. cocoa powder

Instructions:

1) In a bowl combine the cream, mascarpone, Marsala and sugar. Whisk until the cream and mascarpone have the consistency of thickly whipped cream and has strong peaks.

2) In a shallow dish, put the prepared coffee in and dip in a few sponge fingers at a time, turning a few times until they are nicely soaked, but not falling apart. Layer them on your dish until you have used half the biscuits, then spread over half of the cream mixture. Grate the chocolate over the top. Then repeat the layers (you should use up all the coffee), finishing with the creamy layer.

3) Cover and chill until ready to serve. Serve with grated chocolate on top.

Nutritional value: calories: 450, protein: 5, carbohydrates: 37g, fat: 42g, saturates: 30g, fiber: 0g, sugar: 16g, salt: 0.3g

Coconut Covered Orange Chocolate Truffles

Makes 20

Ingredients:

-2 bars organic dark chocolate (70% cocoa)

-2 tbsp. unsalted butter

-Lightly toasted desiccated coconut

-150ml double cream

-1 orange, zest and juice

Instructions:

1.) Break the chocolate into small pieces and tip into a glass bowl.

2.) Meanwhile, in a saucepan combine the double cream and butter on low heat until the butter melts and the cream reaches simmering point. Then, remove from the heat and pour over the chocolate pieces. Stir the chocolate and cream together until the chocolate melts and you get a smooth mixture. Add any flavorings to the truffle mix at this stage, so the orange juice and zest.

3.) Divide the mixture between bowls, then cool and chill in the fridge for at least 4 hrs.

4.) Once chilled, you may now shape the truffles. To do this; you need to dunk a teaspoon in hot water and then scoop up balls of the truffle mix, place the mixture between your palms and roll them into little balls then drop them onto greaseproof paper. If you are struggling to roll them then it may be easier to lightly coat your hands in sunflower oil.

5.) Immediately after rolling, you can coat the truffles in desiccated coconut from a bowl by dropping each rolled truffle into the coating bowl and lightly roll the truffles until evenly coated, then place on greaseproof paper to chill for a further hour.

6.) You can keep the truffles in the fridge for up to 3 days in an air-tight plastic container.

Nutritional value: calories: , protein: 30, carbohydrates: 46g, fat: 22g, saturates: 5g, fiber: 3g, sugar: 1g, salt: 1.1g

One Week Meal Plan

Monday

Breakfast

Scrambled eggs on toast

Cup of coffee or tea

Lunch

Kale Chickpea & Bean Stew

Dinner

Mexican Pot

Dessert

Tiramisu

Tuesday

Breakfast

Multi-Vitamin Smoothie

Cup of coffee or tea

Lunch

Veggie Quinoa Salad with Salmon

Dinner

Chicken Kiev

Dessert

Applesauce Cookies

Wednesday

Breakfast

Omelette

Cup of coffee or tea

Lunch

Creamy Asparagus Pasta

Dinner

Cauliflower Cheese

Dessert

Panna Cotta with Compote

Thursday

Breakfast

Cheese Soufflé

Cup of coffee or tea

Lunch

Sun-Dried Tomatoes Couscous

Dinner

Prawn Style Curry

Dessert

Pear Tarte Tatin

Friday

Breakfast

Blueberry Pancakes

Cup of coffee or tea

Lunch

Chicken Hot Pot

Dinner

Crab Cakes

Dessert

Coconut Covered Orange Chocolate Truffles

Saturday

Breakfast

Flapjack

Cup of coffee or tea

Lunch

Aubergine Slider

Dinner

Orzo Meatballs

Dessert

Apple Strawberry & Macadamia Crumble

Sunday

Breakfast

Berry Porridge Bowl

Cup of coffee or tea

Lunch

Roast Dinner

Dinner

Turkey Casserole

Dessert

Gingerbread Roulade

Conclusion:

Clean eating has so many benefits as we have learnt throughout this book. It is very easy to incorporate more foods from each food group into your current diet or even better, replace it, which will provide you with a delicious plentiful variety. Also, the better you eat the more it has an impact on your overall well-being for example mood is improved, a proven fact. And you'll achieve vibrant skin, improved brain function and you'll feel a lot more energized.

In the recipe section, it is apparent that meals don't have to be boring and bland in order to be healthy. But, instead you'll find you have a more adventurous palette after cooking food yourself, from scratch. You will also discover what quality food tastes like and instead you'll be reaching for the healthier and tastier options rather than processed food.

Limiting packaged and processed food where you can and trying to get back to basics is key to this diet. You will see results in overall health almost immediately after starting this diet plan and hopefully you'll never look back.

Thank you for your time!

Sara Banks

Made in the USA
Middletown, DE
07 April 2016